THE COOLEST JOBS ON THE PLANET

SPECIAL EFFECTS MAKE-UP ARTIST

Jonathan Craig and Bridget Light

Raintree
Chicago, Illinois

To contact Capstone Global Library, please
call 800-747-4992, or visit our web site
www.capstonepub.com

Edited by Nancy Dickmann, Adam Miller,
Laura Knowles, and Helen Cox Cannons
Designed by Richard Parker and Emily Hooton at
Ken Bell Graphic Design
Picture research by Mica Brancic
Production by Vicki Fitzgerald
Printed in the United States of America in
North Mankato, Minnesota.

032019
001726

**Library of Congress Cataloging-in-Publication
Data**
Craig, Jonathan, 1981-
  Special effects make-up artist / Jonathan Craig.
    pages cm.—(The coolest jobs on the planet)
  Includes bibliographical references and index.
  ISBN 978-1-4109-5486-2 (hb)—ISBN 978-1-4109-
5491-6 (pb) 1. Film makeup—Juvenile literature.
2. Theatrical makeup—Juvenile literature. 3.
Television makeup—Juvenile literature. I. Title.

  PN2068.C73 2013
  792'.027—dc23   2012049391

Acknowledgments
We would like to thank the following for
permission to reproduce photographs:
Alamy pp. 9 (© AF Archive), 40 (© David Taylor);
Getty Images pp. 4 (Stone/Ryan McVay), 39
(WireImage/E. Charbonneau); Jonathan Craig
pp. 5, 7, 10, 11, 13, 14, 15, 16, 17, 18 (left & right),
19, 20, 21, 22, 23, 24, 25, 26, 27, 28, 29, 30, 31, 32,
33, 34, 36 bottom, 37 top, 41; Rex Features pp. 6
(Everett Collection), 35 (Moviestore Collection),
38 (Everett Collection); Shutterstock pp. 12 (©
konstantynov), 36 top (© Prezoom.nl), 37 bottom
(© Thorsten Schmitt); The Kobal Collection p. 8
(Columbia).

Background design images supplied by
Shutterstock (© 3d brained,© Attitude, © caesart,
© ChameleonsEye, © dundanim, © Eky Studio, ©
foxie, © Ghenadie, © grivet, © ilolab, © isaravut, ©
IvicaNS, © Jacek Fulawka, © javarman, © Markus
Gann, © Mika Shysh, © Miriam Doerr, © phoebe,
© Skocko, © Steve Collender, © Tjeffersion, ©
twobee, © Vit Kovalcik).

Cover pictures of special-effects artist Steve
Johnson (Ghostbusters, Species) working on
model Mandi Moss of Corbis (ZUMA Press/© Gene Blevins).

Every effort has been made to contact copyright
holders of material reproduced in this book.
Any omissions will be rectified in subsequent
printings if notice is given to the publisher.

CONTENTS

MOVIE MAGIC

Have you ever been scared by a creature you saw in a movie? Have you ever been amazed by the cool makeup in a movie? Have you ever wondered how they do it? I used to wonder the same thing, but now I know the answer, because that is what I do for a living! My name is Jonathan, and I am a special effects make-up artist.

Everybody loves being scared or amazed by a movie.

One of my first jobs was making a real horse look like it was burned for a movie. Even though it was only a student film, it felt so rewarding to see my work on the big screen.

I have a job that is interesting, challenging, and a lot of fun! Nothing compares to transforming an ordinary-looking person into something that only existed in my mind before. Looking back, I could never have imagined making a career out of doing something I love so much. Sometimes following your passion can really pay off. It is never too early to start thinking about what you love to do, and how you can make a living doing it.

MY HERO!
TOM SAVINI (BORN 1946)

Tom Savini did the makeup on some of my favorite horror movies. He came up with brand new techniques and was a big inspiration for me to get into the business. Right after make-up school, I ended up meeting him at a convention. It was pretty awesome.

CHILDHOOD INSPIRATION

As a child, I loved movies with puppets and amazing creatures. My favorites were made by the Jim Henson Creature Shop™. I loved everything they did, from *Sesame Street* and *The Muppet Show* to *Labyrinth* and *Dark Crystal*.

Jim Henson

My father worked in the television industry as a set designer. His job was to find or build the main parts of a set, such as walls and windows, but also smaller details such as background items or props. I remember seeing things in the background of a television program and realizing that my dad had borrowed them from my room. I wondered where my globe had gone!

MY HERO!
JIM HENSON (1936-90)

Not only was Jim Henson the creator of the *Muppets* and *Sesame Street*, but he also voiced and operated many of his creations, most famously Kermit the Frog. He was the first puppeteer to create puppets for television with moving mouths and hands.

On set

One of the productions my dad worked on was called *Under the Umbrella Tree*. It was a children's program that featured puppets like Iggy the Iguana (left), made by Noreen Young. I got to visit my dad on the set, and the highlight of spending time there was meeting Noreen herself and hanging out with the puppeteers. The idea that you could create characters and creatures for television and movies was hugely inspirational for me.

Did you know?

The character Yoda from the *Star Wars* movies *The Empire Strikes Back* (1980) and *Return of the Jedi* (1983) was voiced and puppeted by Frank Oz. Frank Oz often worked with Jim Henson. He was the original puppeteer and voice behind Miss Piggy and Fozzie Bear, among others.

Horror and Halloween

As I got older, I became a big fan of horror movies. I was fascinated by zombies, gore, and aliens. The most fun day of the year for me was always Halloween—and it wasn't just about the free candy! Each year, I wanted to have a scarier costume than the last.

Sometimes my uncle would buy me a make-up kit for Halloween that I could use myself. One year I got a zombie face, while another time it was a skull. Those were the first times I ever created special effects with makeup.

One of my favorite movies when I was young was *Close Encounters of the Third Kind*.

Turtle power!

Probably my favorite costume as a child was when I got to be a Ninja Turtle for Halloween. I did not make that one myself—we bought it at the store—but the original *Teenage Mutant Ninja Turtles* movie (1990) was a huge inspiration for me. In the movie, the costume was a suit and head that the actor wore. The heads had animatronics (when electronics are used to animate a creature) to move the facial features. It was a crazy concept, but it worked!

The costumes from the original *Teenage Mutant Ninja Turtles* really brought those characters to life.

ESSENTIAL SKILLS

Every movie or character starts with an idea. If you have an active imagination, you have the ability to come up with great ideas. Turning imagination into reality is what being a make-up artist is all about.

Did you know?

The Jim Henson Creature Shop™ made the costumes for the original *Teenage Mutant Ninja Turtles* movie and its sequel, *Teenage Mutant Ninja Turtles II: The Secret of the Ooze* (1991). No wonder I loved them so much!

A LIFE-CHANGING DECISION

Here I am shooting a movie in Los Angeles.

In high school, in Ottawa, Canada, I volunteered as a camera operator through a program at a local television station. They trained me and gave me the opportunity to shoot live music, sports, and local events. It eventually became a paying job, and I was able to branch out and work for other stations.

I really enjoyed filming, and by the time I graduated from high school, I had decided that my career would be operating a camera for television. After a few more years working in Ottawa, I moved to Toronto, also in Canada. In a larger city, there were more opportunities.

This is my friend Eric's Halloween costume. Even though I did the makeup myself, he creeped me out all night!

TOOLS OF THE TRADE:
PROSTHETIC TEETH

Prosthetic teeth like these can be made in the studio to fit an actor's mouth or they can be ordered online. Teeth are one of the things that we recognize people by. Just changing people's teeth can make them look like entirely different people.

Looking for something new

My job as a camera operator was exciting—I got to travel and film interesting things. But I never stopped thinking about puppets, monsters, and makeup. One day, I decided to look into taking a class. I didn't necessarily think this would be a new career path; I just wanted to be able to create frightening and believable Halloween makeup and masks for myself and my friends.

Make-up school

I found that there were several certificate courses available. Certificate courses are not as broad as a college degree. They are generally shorter and more intensive, and you earn a certificate upon completion.

I finally chose the School of Professional Makeup. It offered the shortest program (four months), which was great for me because I didn't want to be out of work for too long. Most importantly, many of the instructors were people who had worked on my favorite horror movies!

ESSENTIAL SKILLS

Shading and color blending are important skills, because a make-up artist needs to be able to create depth and shape in a natural-looking way.

Although I have never used my beauty or bridal makeup skills professionally, I could still do it, especially if it was for a zombie bride!

Here comes the bride...?

To take the Prosthetic and Special FX make-up class, you first have to learn beauty and bridal makeup. Although I didn't really have any interest in this kind of makeup, I was willing to do whatever was required to get to the point where I could learn how to do monster and zombie makeup.

After completing the beauty course, I realized it is important for every make-up artist to know the basics. I learned how to match skin tones, cover imperfections, and use highlighting and shadowing to emphasize certain features. All these skills are important when creating creature makeup.

The first time I felt like a real artist was when I got my own set of make-up brushes.

TOOLS OF THE TRADE: MAKE-UP BRUSHES

It is important to keep your brushes clean, since they are expensive to replace. I have large brushes for applying powder and blush, small, thin brushes for creating veins and other fine details, and everything in between.

Special effects and prosthetics

In the special effects part of the make-up class, I learned how to make prosthetics. A make-up prosthetic is something applied to a person that gives the illusion that it is actually part of his or her body. It can be as simple as a mole or as complicated as an entire creature that barely looks human.

This was my first special effects project for the class.

Getting the design right

The first thing I was taught is that character design is very important! Special effects make-up artists need to have information about the character they are trying to create. It could be a sketch, a photograph, or just a written description. Often, the make-up artists come up with a sketch themselves, based on discussions with the creator. Imagination and the ability to sketch can be great assets here.

No prosthetics required

During this part of the class, I also learned a number of out-of-kit techniques using simply makeup, paint, and wax that can be used to transform someone into a particular character. My class got to visit the set of a television program to watch professional make-up artists in action.

TOOLS OF THE TRADE: PORTFOLIO

A portfolio is a collection of your past work—usually photographs. Special FX make-up artists need to build a good portfolio to get work. You can start working on your portfolio in college.

MY HEROES! MATT DEWILDE, ALLAN COOKE, AND RANDY DAUDLIN

Matt DeWilde and Allan Cooke were my prosthetic teachers at school. They are both talented sculptors and make-up artists who not only taught me my craft, but also helped me find work. Randy Daudlin was my out-of-kit teacher. I learned so much from him, too.

Matt DeWilde

I was very inspired by my teachers, including Matt DeWilde, because they were earning a living doing what I really wanted to do.

STARTING OFF

Through the school, I was able to find some jobs. Though they were unpaid or low paying, they allowed me to build my portfolio. One of them was doing a burned horse (see page 5) for a college film, and another was a music video featuring flying monkeys. It was a spoof of *The Wizard of Oz* (1939). I had a great time doing it, and it really boosted my confidence knowing that I could pull off something that was really challenging.

Did you know?

The Wizard of Oz was the first movie that used foam-latex for the prosthetics. The Scarecrow, the Tin Man, the Cowardly Lion, the Wicked Witch of the West, and the Flying Monkeys all had latex features attached to them. Foam-latex is still commonly used today.

These flying monkeys are from the music video I worked on.

I still do Halloween makeup for friends today. It is a great opportunity for me to try out my latest prosthetic or practice a new technique.

Even better zombies

I was also excited to finally be able to do really professional Halloween makeup for my friends and myself. When I first started out, Halloween was a great time to practice things I had learned in school. I made some of my friends into zombies or gave them broken noses. These were really fun to do, and I was able to use the pictures for my portfolio!

Making a living

The movie industry is a competitive business. I know many people who make a living by being make-up artists, but many of us have other jobs as well. For example, I still operate cameras for television to help pay the bills. But even if I go a while without doing makeup on a production, I am still working in my workshop. It is very important for me to keep my skills up-to-date, so I'm always trying new techniques and playing with new materials.

My latest project is sculpting a puppet based on a drawing by my sister. I hope to use this in my own production one day.

TOOLS OF THE TRADE: SCULPTING TOOLS

Sculpting tools, such as trowels and scrapers, are used to get different texture effects on the clay. Spray bottles are used to keep water-based clay moist.

Here is a tool for cutting clay. Every job needs a different tool.

A family affair

I come from a family of artists. After being a set designer for many years, my dad followed his passion and became a successful painter. My mother has made jewelry and owned her own animation studio. Like my dad, my sister also makes her living as a painter, and my brother is a professional photographer. There are definite ups and downs working in a creative field, but it really helps to have my family—we have always supported each other in all our endeavors.

MATERIALS

One of my favorite things to do as a make-up artist is play with gloop! There are so many different kinds of materials used in prosthetic makeup. Some of the main materials I work with are clay, concrete, alginate, silicon, gelatin, latex, foam, and foam-latex.

Here are a few of the materials that I use.

Some materials, such as clay, are used for sculpting. Others, such as concrete and alginate, are used to build molds. The actual prosthetics that are adhered (stuck) to an actor might be made from silicon, gelatin, or foam-latex. All these materials start off as goo or powder, but they end up making something amazing!

Safety first!

Many of the materials used in FX makeup are toxic, so it is very important when working with certain chemicals to have the right safety equipment. It is also important to make sure that any actor having a prosthetic applied is not allergic to any of the materials.

Did you know?

Silicon is the second most abundant element in our planet's crust. Many silicone products are made using the element silicon, including cookware, contact lenses, medical scar treatments, sealant products for buildings, and even shampoos and hair gels. The silicone I use comes in a two-part clear liquid, which turns to rubber when mixed together. There are hundreds of different kinds of silicone, and certain jobs call for certain types. Originally, they were all created from silicon dioxide.

These are some of the things that keep me safe when I'm working with toxic chemicals. I also make sure the studio is well ventilated.

latex gloves

safety goggles

gas mask for handling toxic chemicals

A WEEK IN THE LIFE

Every project is different, but many can be worked on over a number of days. For this project, I was asked to create a large prosthetic nose. The nose would be used in a television program that was conducting an experiment to see how real people would treat an actress based on the size of her nose.

Here, my friend Christina (another talented make-up artist) and I are casting the actress's face.

Day 1: Casting a face

The actress playing the part came to my studio to have her face cast. My assistant and I cast her face using alginate (a powder mixed with water that hardens) and plaster bandage (which also hardens when wet—it is often used for casts for broken legs or arms). Once everything had hardened, I carefully removed the material.

Now I had a perfect negative of her face. That means once concrete is poured into it, I could create an exact copy of her face. I created the concrete copy to have a base for sculpting what would be the prosthetic nose. That way, it would fit over her actual face exactly.

Once the concrete has been poured into the mold, we all must wait for it to harden.

negative

concrete copy

Note to self

Always have an assistant when casting a face. Assistants can keep an eye out to make sure that the alginate does not block someone's nasal passage and stop him or her from breathing.

Did you know?

Alginate is extracted from seaweed. It doesn't taste like sushi, though! Some alginate is actually flavored like mint for use when casting teeth. If you have braces, your dentist probably cast your teeth with alginate first.

Day 2: Sculpting the nose

Using clay, I sculpted a new nose on top of the concrete face cast. It is always a good idea to work from photos or sketches of the prosthetic you are trying to create. For more complicated makeup, I would spend a lot of time researching the concept, but for this project I found a photo online of a large nose and worked from that.

The clay is sculpted onto the concrete face.

Making a mold

Once I'd sculpted the nose to my satisfaction, I was ready to move to the next step, which was creating a mold of the new nose. To make the mold, I built a wall around the face and poured in concrete. The wall is only needed until the concrete has set.

Concrete molds take about an hour to harden, so sometimes you can start making prosthetics the same day. In this case, I left it to harden overnight. The next morning, I opened the mold and removed the clay. What was left was the concrete negative of the nose that I sculpted. I was then ready to make the actual prosthetic that the actress would wear.

Here is the two-part nose mold fitted together, with one part on top of the other.

TOOLS OF THE TRADE: DREMEL

A Dremel can be used for cutting, sanding, and polishing different materials. For the nose mold, I used the Dremel to make three holes. When you make the second part of the mold, cement fills the three holes, and they act as keys or indicators of where the mold fits together.

Note to self

Clay can be used for more than just sculpting. Use it to build the walls for a mold, and remember to reuse old clay.

Day 3: Making the prosthetic

For this project, I used gelatin to create the prosthetic, because it sets quickly and is cheaper than some other materials. It is important to consider the budget when deciding what materials to use, and this television program didn't have a large budget.

There are downsides to using gelatin. The prosthetic cannot be reused, and if it gets too hot, it will start to soften and can fall off the actor's face! This shoot was only for one day, so it wasn't necessary for the prosthetic to be reused.

To make the prosthetic, I heated up the gelatin in the microwave until it became a liquid, and then I poured it into the negative of the nose. I then pressed the second part of the mold (the concrete face cast) into it and squeezed them tightly together.

Be patient!

Gelatin takes about 20 minutes to set, and it is very important to wait until it does. If you open it too soon, you can ruin the prosthetic. Once the gelatin had set, I removed the new prosthetic nose, and it was then ready to be fitted to the actress's face.

Note to self

Be very careful handling materials. For example, hot gelatin can burn your skin.

This is the finished nose!

ESSENTIAL SKILL

Being able to make a mold correctly is a key skill. It must be strong, clean, and, most importantly, a mold that opens up! If you do not make the seam in the correct location, both sides of the mold can lock together and never open. Then you have to start

Day 4: Applying the prosthetic

It was finally time to go on set and transform the actress. On the previous day, I had made five noses. I nearly always make more prosthetics than I need, because if the edges are not perfect or something goes wrong with the application, I need to have backups, especially because gelatin prosthetics cannot be reused.

I brought the three noses that turned out the best and, using prosthetic glue, I attached the best one onto the actress's real nose. I smoothed out the edges and used a solvent to dissolve them seamlessly into the skin. Once the nose was properly applied, I painted the prosthetic to match her natural skin color.

Applying a nose to an actress on set is a tricky job.

TOOLS OF THE TRADE: MAKE-UP REMOVER

Part of a make-up artist's job includes removing makeup when the filming is finished. Some prosthetic glue is very strong, and trying to take off a prosthetic without make-up remover could injure the actor.

The final product— success!

Too hot to handle

I planned the application to take 30 to 45 minutes, but because the lights were so hot, the actress was sweating, and the prosthetic started to become soft. The first two noses ripped, and I had to be extremely careful with the last one—but, luckily, everything went well.

Day 5: Out-of kit makeup

Some prosthetic makeup is done entirely out of kit, which means that it doesn't involve a pre-made appliance or prosthetic. On set, I have to create a character or wound with whatever I have brought with me. I might use paints, makeup, and wax to create 3D wounds such as a broken nose or cut.

Wax is a great material to create different effects. It works well for wounds, because it is like adding a new layer of skin that you can then paint over—it is easy to make it appear like the skin has ripped. The effects you can get just using paint and makeup are amazing. You can make a nose look broken and swollen with highlights and shadow alone and no 3D prosthetic.

This makeup was done entirely out of kit. Paint and makeup can be used to make someone look dirty, tired, older, or more glamorous.

Good hair day

On set, character makeup can also involve hair. I may have to apply a fake moustache or maybe a bald cap. Before I go on set, I figure out what kind of effect I will need to create and make sure I have the proper tools and materials needed.

Here are some of the items I take on set with me.

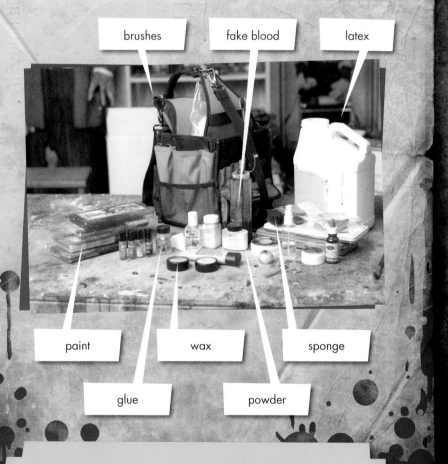

brushes

fake blood

latex

paint

wax

sponge

glue

powder

TOOLS OF THE TRADE: AIRBRUSH

An airbrush is really useful. You spray on makeup using an air compressor, which spreads it finely enough to achieve a seamless transition of color. It is excellent for highlights and shadows.

WHEN THINGS GO WRONG

Doing prosthetic makeup is a complicated process, and there are plenty of opportunities for things to go wrong along the way. I have opened molds too early, broken molds, and mixed chemicals incorrectly so that they didn't set properly. Although I know I will continue to make mistakes, I always learn from them.

The mold broke—disaster!

A problem nose

With the gelatin nose prosthetic that I worked on, I actually dropped the original nose sculpture that I had been working on for several hours. I had to start sculpting it again from scratch! Luckily, because I started the project early, I had the time to redo it.

The edges on this makeup are too visible. Back to the drawing board!

ESSENTIAL SKILL

You need to be clever and inventive to solve problems. On one movie set, the script was changed at the last minute, and they needed to make it look like a part of someone's head had been shot off. I hadn't planned for this, but I got some wax and blood from my kit and some pieces of plastic I found around the set and was able to create something that looked very realistic.

Note to self

Don't panic! It can make a bad situation worse. On one occasion, I was making a wound that had to bleed. The blood was held inside a latex bladder (similar to a balloon, but much thinner) underneath a skin prosthetic. This was a last-minute project, and all the bladders I'd made the night before failed. I had to stay up all night remaking them. I ended up pulling it off because I stayed calm and kept going.

DEVELOPING SKILLS

Growing up watching my favorite movies, I thought makeup and prosthetics were done by people who were more talented and creative than I was. It wasn't until later on in life that I realized I could actually learn how to do this, too.

While in school, I learned some important tricks of the trade. But there are also additional classes that you can take, such as life drawing or sculpting, or classes on specific techniques like airbrushing. Make-up conventions are a great place to learn about new products and meet people in the same profession.

Here I am practicing sculpting.

Practice makes perfect!

The most important thing I have done is to continue practicing what I have learned. The more you do things, the better you get. I will never stop learning or practicing.

MY HERO!
VE NEIL (BORN 1951)

I am a longtime fan of Tim Burton movies, and one of my favorites as a child was *Beetlejuice* (1988). The makeup, creatures, and effects in that movie have always inspired me. The make-up artist Ve Neil won an Academy Award for her work on *Beetlejuice*. She has also won Academy Awards for *Mrs. Doubtfire* (1993) and *Ed Wood* (1994). Recently, she did the makeup for *The Hunger Games* (2012).

Beetlejuice

ESSENTIAL SKILL

To be successful, you need to be able to motivate yourself to work on your own projects and keep practicing your skills, even when you're not working for someone else. It is also important to work on promoting yourself and making connections. Sometimes this business can be discouraging, since there is a lot of competition, so it's important to be able to persevere through the tough times.

Puppets and eyeballs

To keep motivated, I spend a lot of my free time working on my own projects. One of the things I really love doing is using my FX skills to make puppets. Unlike traditional fabric puppets (like the Muppets or Fraggles), the puppets I create are usually made from silicon and are more life-like. I love creating a character and making up my own story about him or her. Often, I will make a short film featuring that character.

These are a number of my puppets—all personal projects.

MY HERO! RICK BAKER (BORN 1950)

Rick Baker is one of the all-time great special effects make-up artists. He has won Academy Awards for seven movies, including *The Nutty Professor* (1996) and *How the Grinch Stole Christmas* (2000).

Many of my masks and puppets need eyes, so I have spent a lot of time making artificial eyeballs. Making them look realistic is very difficult!

It's alive!

Some of these puppets are operated by hand and some by rods and cabletronics. If you plan to create a moving creature, it is good to learn about animatronics. You can give something a fairly complex range of motion, such as moving eyes or fingers, using cables and pulleys. It works in a similar way to brakes on a bicycle.

Did anyone ask for a severed arm?

Other projects I work on in my own time are masks, body parts, teeth, and things that may end up being useful for upcoming productions. I never know when someone might call needing a severed arm for a war movie!

Did you know?

Artificial eyes were originally made out of glass. Although some are still made in this way today, it is more usual to make them out of acrylics or resins.

HISTORY OF SPECIAL EFFECTS MAKEUP

Using makeup for theatrical effect has been around for a long time, centuries before movies were invented in the 1890s, but with the beginnings of movies, new ideas and innovations began to change things. In the early part of the 1900s, movie actors did their own makeup.

An early innovator of FX makeup was an actor named Lon Chaney. He starred in many classic movies, including *The Hunchback of Notre Dame* (1923) and *Phantom of the Opera* (1925). He earned the nickname "man with a thousand faces" for his ability to transform himself using makeup.

Jack Pierce

MY HERO!
JACK PIERCE (1889-1968)

Jack Pierce was renowned for his out-of-kit makeup ability. He created the original Frankenstein, in addition to creating the makeup for other iconic movies such as *The Mummy* (1932) and *The Wolf Man* (1941).

Using computers

In the early 1990s, CG (which stands for "computer generated") effects became popular. Things that were once done with makeup and props were now being done with computer animation. In recent years, however, special effects makeup and practical effects (ones that are not computer generated) have made a real comeback.

Ralph Fiennes played Lord Voldemort in the Harry Potter movies.

CG may be quicker and less expensive, but it does have limitations to how realistic it can look. These days, both CG effects and make-up effects are combined to get the best of both worlds. A good example of this is Ralph Fiennes as Lord Voldemort in the *Harry Potter* movies. The makeup is real, but his nose is digitally removed.

Did you know?

Make-up artists had to apply Harry Potter's lightning bolt-shaped scar approximately 5,800 times over the course of eight movies.

WHAT YOU CAN DO NOW

If you are interested in becoming a special effects make-up artist one day, or even if you just think it would be cool to do some of this stuff for fun, it is pretty easy to get started. The Internet is an excellent resource for make-up tips and tricks, but the most important thing is to practice sketching and sculpting your ideas. Even if you are just using modeling clay, you would be surprised by what you can come up with. I once made a pretty realistic prosthetic finger out of play dough!

Why not try out some makeup on a friend?

ESSENTIAL SKILL

You need to be able to sketch and to get across your ideas to a potential client. People hiring you will usually want to see what you can do before they pay you for it. This is another great reason to have a good portfolio.

Basic equipment

There are sculpting and mold-making kits for beginners available online or at fine art and craft shops. Make-up stores and costume stores will have starter make-up kits, or you can get some makeup and soft wax and bring your own ideas to life. There is probably even stuff around your house that you could use.

Taking art classes in school, or even outside of school to gain additional knowledge, can give you a head start. I wish I had taken more classes when I was younger.

paper

clay

pencils

brushes

Note to self

Don't be afraid to try out your ideas—get messy, have fun, and see where your creativity can take you!

QUIZ

See if you have what it takes to become a special effects make-up artist.

1. What do you most prefer to do in your spare time?

    a) Do something active such as playing basketball or jogging.

    b) Draw, paint, or sculpt.

    c) Play video and computer games or watch TV.

2. What kind of job do you think you would like to have?

    a) Something with a predictable schedule and income; doing the same job at the same place.

    b) Something creative and hands on; contract work with an unpredictable schedule; always doing something new.

    c) Something with a flexible schedule that you control; being your own boss.

3. If you were working on a movie, what would you like to do?

    a) Act—I love to be the center of attention.

    b) Makeup and effects—I'm a very visual and creative person.

    c) Direct—I like to be in charge.

    d) Write—I'm creative and like to come up with stories.

4. If you're faced with a challenge when working on a project, how do you usually react?

    a) Get frustrated and give up.

    b) Stay calm and try to work through the problem.

    c) Get panicky and have a meltdown.

5. Do you think you would enjoy working on projects with lots of complicated steps that take a while to complete?

   a) No—I get distracted easily and like to see quick results.

   b) Yes—I love a project with many steps. It feels like a real accomplishment when I'm finished.

   c) Not sure—I probably wouldn't mind if I really liked the project.

If you answered mostly Bs, it is a good indication that special effects makeup could be a great career for you!

GLOSSARY

acrylic in special effects makeup, a hard plastic used for making things like teeth prosthetics

alginate powder that is mixed with water to create a gooey substance that hardens in air. It is mainly used for making casts.

animatronics technique of making and operating lifelike robots , usually for film or television

CG (computer generated) use of computer graphics to create images and effects added to art, video games, or movies

convention show or meeting. Depending on the convention, there may be people selling products, doing demonstrations, or speaking about certain topics.

Dremel rotary tool that has changeable heads (bits). Depending on the bit, it can be used to drill, sharpen, polish, and so on.

foam-latex soft, lightweight foam used to make prosthetics, it is formed when certain chemicals are added to latex

gelatin food product that is also used in FX makeup to create prosthetics

latex natural latex is a milky fluid that comes from plants and is used to make rubber. Latex can also be made synthetically.

mold block hollowed out into a shape. The mold is filled with a substance like gelatin or foam latex. When the substance hardens, the mold is opened, and the substance is shaped exactly like the hollowed-out area.

negative in the case of a mold, the negative would be the hollowed-out area, whereas the positive would be the prosthetic created by the mold

out-of-kit effects effects that you create on the spot using paints, makeup, or waxes, rather than on any premade prosthetics

portfolio collection of work, usually documented by photographs, that can be easily shown to clients

prosthetic in makeup, a prosthetic is something applied to a person that gives the illusion that it is actually part of his or her body

resin thick liquid that hardens into a solid substance, often transparent. Resins can be natural or synthetic.

set designer person whose job it is to create the look of a set. A set could be a room, a studio, a stage, or an outdoor space—any place where a production takes place.

silicone in FX makeup, two liquid substances are mixed to create silicone. Once hardened, it has a consistency similar to gelatin. It is used to create lifelike skin texture for application as a prosthetic or as a lifelike prop.

solvent substance that dissolves another substance. For example, witch hazel is a solvent for gelatin.

special effects (FX) in TV or movies, making something look real or believable without actually having to do it for real

toxic damaging to a living organism, such as a plant or animal. If a substance is toxic to humans, it means that it could make you sick or, if it is extremely toxic, cause death.

FIND OUT MORE

Books

Colson, Mary. *Being a Makeup Artist* (On the Radar: Awesome Jobs). Minneapolis: Lerner, 2013.

Daudlin, Randy. *Reel Characters*. Markdale, Ont.: Two Gruesome, 2010.

Debreceni, Todd. *Special Makeup Effects for Stage and Screen: Making and Applying Prosthetics*. Burlington, Mass.: Focal Press, 2012.

Horn, Geoffrey M. *Movie Makeup, Costumes, and Sets* (Making Movies). Milwaukee: G. Stevens Publishing, 2007.

Svitil, Torene, and Amy Dunkleberger. *So You Want to Work in Set Design, Costuming, or Make-Up?* (Careers in Film and Television). Berkeley Heights, N.J.: Enslow, 2008.

Web sites

www.dicksmithmake-up.com

Dick Smith has worked as a make-up artist for 60 years and has won an Academy Award for Lifetime Achievement. You can see pictures of some of his creations on his web site.

www.kidzworld.com/article/6096-halloween-make-up-tips

Learn how to create some basic Halloween makeup on this site.

www.makeupfxtech.com

This web site features lots of interesting videos and information about the special effects makeup used in a variety of popular television shows, movies, music videos, and more. The site also features tutorial videos that show you how to achieve different effects.

Places to visit

International Make-Up Artist Trade Show

www.imats.net

This convention features talks from the world's top make-up artists as well as displays and demonstrations showing all the latest tools and techniques. Visit the show's web site to see if it will take place in a city near you.

Museum of the Moving Image

36-01 35 Avenue (at 37 Street)

Astoria, New York 11106

www.movingimage.us

Visit the Museum of the Moving Image to see some amazing objects and films connected to movie history.

Topics for further research

Why not try experimenting with makeup on your friends? Perhaps you could turn them into something scary for Halloween, or—if it's not that time of year—turn them into an animal, such as a lion? You can buy face-paint kits (including fake blood!) for a reasonable price, and it can be a good starting point in learning how to use makeup. Always make sure that you ask permission from an adult before using makeup.

INDEX

DO YOU LIKE MOVIES? HOW ABOUT ZOMBIES AND ALIENS?

MAYBE YOU COULD CREATE YOUR OWN WEIRD AND WONDERFUL MOVIE CREATURES!

ignite

Jonathan Craig has created everything from puppets to flying monkeys for films and television. In this book you'll find out all about his amazing job!

Other books about cool jobs:

THE COOLEST JOBS ON THE PLANET
MARS ROVER DRIVER

THE COOLEST JOBS ON THE PLANET
WILDLIFE PHOTOGRAPHER

THE COOLEST JOBS ON THE PLANET
Computer Games Designer

Level U

ISBN 978-1-4109-5491-6

90000

Heinemann
Raintree

a capstone imprint   www.capstonepub.com

9 781410 954916